OPC2023A

Black Eyes Publishing UK & Gloucestershire Poetry Society
Open Poetry Competition 2023 Anthology

OPC2023A

Black Eyes Publishing UK & Gloucestershire Poetry Society
Open Poetry Competition 2023 Anthology

Black Eyes Publishing UK

OPC2023A
© Gloucestershire Poetry Society 2023

Published 2023
Black Eyes Publishing UK
Gloucester GL1 3ET (UK)

www.blackeyespublishinguk.co.uk

ISBN: 978-1-913195-27-4

All poems in this anthology remain within the copyright of the individual poets. They have asserted their moral right under the Copyright, Designs and Patents Act, 1988, to be identified as the authors of their work.

All Rights reserved. No part of this publication may be reproduced, copied, stored in a retrieval system, or transmitted, in any form or by any means, without the prior written consent of the copyright holder(s), nor be otherwise circulated in any form of binding or cover other than that in which it is published and without a similar condition being imposed on the subsequent purchaser.

A CIP catalogue record for this title is available from the British Library.

Editor: Peter Lay

www.thegloucestershirepoetrysociety.com

Cover design: Jason Conway, The Daydream Academy.
www.thedaydreamacademy.com

Introduction

It gives me great pleasure to introduce this anthology *OPC2023A* of poems from **The Black Eyes, Gloucestershire Poetry Society (GPS) 2023 Open Poetry Competition**. The total entry for the 2023 competition was 568 poems, with all entries being considered anonymously, throughout the process.

Longlisting was undertaken by Josephine Lay (Former Dir. Of Ops for the GPS & lead editor for Black Eyes Publishing) with assistance from Jason Conway (Current Dir. Of Ops for the GPS). The Longlist consisted of 77 poems. All longlisted poems were eligible for this anthology. However, several eligible poems, were withdrawn, once the results had been announced, to be either submitted elsewhere, or re-worked.

The Longlist was judged by Jessica Mookherjee (her judges report is included in this anthology) Jessica produced a Shortlist of 21 poems, before settling on the final results.

The GPS Friendship Prize was judged by Josephine, from the 75 poems submitted to **The Black Eyes, Gloucestershire Poetry Society (GPS) 2023 Open Poetry Competition,** by GPS Friendship Members. Josephine's judges report is included in this anthology, together with the poems included in the results.

Finally, many thanks, and congratulations on their choices to the judges.

Peter Lay
Black Eyes Publication UK
December 2023

Contents

9	**Black Eyes/GPS 2023 Open Poetry Competition** **Judges Report: Jessica Mookherjee**
11	**GPS Friendship Prize** **Judges Report: Josephine Lay**
13	**A Commuter Works at Home in the Village** – Christopher Horton
14	**A dish served cold** – Daphne M. Larner
16	**After The Moon** – Sally Aspden
17	**A is ?** – Alan Mansell
18	**A long way down the road** – Claire James
19	**and when the children vomited** – Owen Gallagher
20	**Anglerfish** – Carol Sheppard
21	**Aubade** – Vicky Hampton
22	**Be Still, But Never Stop** – Emma Lord
23	**Becoming Eve** – Margaret Royall
24	**Black Crow laughing in the city heat** – Jean Grimsey
25	**BOUND** – Frank MacMahon
26	**Brontë Falls** – Alice Brooker
27	**Church Gone** – David J. Costello
29	**Code Talkers 1** – Vivian E. Badoni
30	**Cost of Austerity** – Nigel Kent
31	**Crow** – Emma Lord
33	**Dad** – Dani Hawkes
34	**Dear Merthyr** – Lisa Kelly
35	**Dear Poetry, last night I dreamt I spoke with my father** – Anna Saunders
37	**Rating Goat Curry** – Jenny Mitchell
39	**Falling for the moon** – Catherine Baker
40	**Fardel's Bear** – Allan Lake
41	**Gloria holds my hand *en San Bernardino*** – Linda Ravenswood
42	**I am me** – B. Anne Adriaens
44	**...in alignment** – Simon Alderwick
45	**In the November square, Kherson** – Tess Biddington
47	**Knotted Ribbon** – Charlotte Murray
48	**Learning to sing** – Estelle Price
50	**Lexicon** – Jodie Duffy
51	**Meteors In The Night** – Stuti Sinha
52	**Midsummer's Day, Orkney** – Julie-Ann Rowell

53	**Nest** – Catherine Baker
55	**Nightfall in Nairobi** – Estelle Price
56	**No Country** – Sharon Savory
57	**Ode to Women Wielding Swords** – Iris Anne Lewis
58	**Philip Larkin meets Josephine Baker** – Emma Conally-Barklem
59	**Postlude** – James Lilliefors
61	**PUTIN AND ME** – Paul Francis
63	**Rainbows on the Shore** – Sharon Savory
64	**Raking for the Moon** – Sue Finch
66	**Reveal** – Charlie Markwick
67	**sky of los Feliz** – Linda Ravenswood
68	**Slow Dancer** – Charlotte Faulconbridge
69	**SOLDIER** - Melvin Palowski Moore (Silver Lion Poet)
70	**speech therapy** – Simon Alderwick
72	**Station to Station** – Dominic James
74	**Strict and Immovable** – Alan Dunnett
75	**The Birdscarer** – David Hale
77	**The Comfort of Crumbs** – Nigel Kent
78	**The Effects of Rage** – Jane Burn
79	**The mirror turns** – Estelle Price
80	**The Music Box** – Annie Ellis
81	**The Scarf** – Annie Ellis
82	**there's all the blue and all the green** – Suzy Aspell
83	**This** – Scott Elder
84	**THOUGHTS** – Clive Oseman
85	**TOADSTOOL, FROG'S UMBRELLA** - Isabella Mead
87	**Tomorrow I will Grieve for my Country** – Anne Sheppard
88	**Two Mirrors** – Maria Roe
89	**We dug a hole** - Charlotte Stokes Meyer zu Natrup
90	**Wimblebarrow** – David Hale
91	**Wing Mirror Love Song - A golden shovel after Bob Dylan** - Jane Spray
93	**Words Fail** – Greg Smith

Black Eyes/GPS 2023 Open Poetry Competition

Judges Report: Jessica Mookherjee - Author of *Tigress* (Nine Arches Press – shortlisted for Ledbury Munthe Prize 2021) and *Notes from the Shipwreck* (Nine Arches Press 2022) and *Desire Lines* (Broken Sleep Books 2023). Co-Editor of Against the Grain Press.

It is always a pleasure to judge poetry competitions because of the unexpected and varied nature of the poems that come to you. It is also an honour, because you are in the presence of people's creations that have come out moving and rich experiences. It is also a very difficult and almost impossible task, because at one level – all art is subjective to taste. However when looking for the winning poems among all the worthy long list, I asked myself some fundamental questions. The first set of questions were about the difficult arena of craft and the last couple of questions were about emotion and impact. For a poet walks those lines between craft and art as well as performance.

I asked firstly; is this form working for this poem and this subject? There were many great poems sent in where the poem wasn't fully living in the form the poet had given it. It's always a good idea to ask if a particular form might help the subject matter. There were some poems where the form dominated the poem. There were many poems about fathers sent in and it made me think of Dylan Thomas's Do Not Go Gentle poem, where he uses a villanelle to emphasise repetition and change. Poetry is often perfect vehicle for this and for saying the unsayable, fusing thoughts that just wouldn't work in say, a song or a story. There were a few poems that were so moving, particularly about grief, poverty and stories of ancestors but just fell short of the shortlist because there needed a bit more movement in them. It is always good to ask ourselves why this form, why a poem and not a song or a short story? One of the highly commended poems *Eating Curry Goat* is a great example of how the form works for and with the poem, it doesn't need to be formal to have form. Another is *Strict and Immovable*, where the collaged and fragmented nature of the form and word choices added so much weight to the subject matter.

Secondly I asked is this poem finished? – has it the best edit possible for it to fly into the world? There were such beautiful poems sent in, ones of love, and I am pleased to say – many poems about politics and power. All of the poems I read had some excellent and stand out lines, however some poems could have been edited further to pull out that power. For one or two poems in the long list – I wanted just that bit more, for some a little less. It is important to write about the ills of the world and our anger in the midst of powerlessness. I want to commend all poets who wrote about injustice, politics, conflict and climate.

Thirdly I asked – is this poem surprising and unexpected? It is always with a sense of awe of the human psyche that I read a poem, bearing witness to a person's weight of emotion in words. All of the long-listed poems were ones that needed to be written. It is when a poem makes me see something I have never seen, or shocks me or even pushes me beyond my first reaction that I return to the poem, over and over. It was great to read so many love poems, we need more love in the world most definitely, but how do we love? The love described in the highly commended *Sky of Los Feliz* had me gripped.

Finally I asked myself does this poem make me cry, laugh, howl, or even wince. What does the poem do to me? Every poem in the long list had an impact on me and every poem on the short list made me want to return to the emotions and go deeper. From the poignant/funny of the love letter to Merthyr, with the fabulous tilt and lilt of the language and that all too familiar feeling of not quite being home to the fear and loathing of Putin and Me, all of these poems wove language and emotion together. There were so many great poems about the use of language and tongue. I thought I had found my winner early, but when I got to the eventual winner, I kept returning to **We Dug a Hole** over and over again – its sheer exuberance and confidence left me breathless. Well done to the poet, as they have shown what the English language can do and also said something to me about the confusing times we live in too- how we can be twisted and turned. The runner up, and by not much in it – was **Gloria holds my hand en San Bernardino**, how I fell in love with this poem, the arc and sweep and majesty of it and again, its mastery of language and the cinematic textures, I was with Gloria. I have often wondered what would happen if **Philip Larkin meets Josephine Baker**, I joke, I have never wondered this – but now after reading the poem I am thinking about the complexity of the nineteen twenties and Larkin's poem 'For Sydney Bechet'. I am also applauding all the poet's bravery to tackle difficult subjects because it only when we start these debates do we get a good dialogue about race, poetry, language, performance, the world we find ourselves in, what is acceptable, who we are and our relationship to a bigger world.

Well done to all poets on the list and well done to everyone who entered because you keep community poetry and the poets and yourself going and huge well done to the winner, as I am now just a little bit in love with you. *JM*

The Gloucestershire Poetry Society Friendship Prize
(from entries by members of the Gloucestershire Poetry Society Friendship Group)

Judges report: Josephine Lay – was Dir. of Ops. for The Gloucestershire Poetry Society for three years and regularly hosted 'Crafty Crows'; a monthly online poetry event. Prior to the pandemic she hosted Squawkers in Cheltenham. She, is the author of three poetry collections: *Inside Reality* (2018), *Unravelling* (2019) and *A Quietus* (2021) as well as a novel *Creating Stanley* (2022) and a collection of short stories *Saffron Tones* (2017). Josephine is the editor for Black Eyes Pubblishing.

This year, both the long listing of the GPS Open Poetry Competition, and the judging of the Friendship Prize, were challenging. There were many poems that caught my attention, some lyrical, some sharp on the page, some full of images and some that brought tears. I was very glad to hand the long list over to Jessica Mukherjee. But then there remained the judging of the Friendship Prize (75 poems) of which 10 lovely poems became a personal short-list, but there could only be one winner of the prize and it had to be **'In the November Square, Kherson'**. This poem placed me, both visually and emotionally, in that recently occupied, and then recaptured, Ukrainian City of Kherson. The poetry was tight, cleverly executed and well placed on the page. I found myself reading it over and over again, finding a new nuance/insight each time.

There were other poems that moved me and were close runners up: *'No Country'*, leads the reader into the experience of being mixed race in Britain today. *'Aubade'* was lyrical and beautiful; using music as a metaphor for a waning love affair. *'After the Moon'* caught my eye with its shining lake, and finally, a mention for *'The Scarf'* of dragonflies between folds of fabric. Lovely. *JL*

Longlisted, Shortlisted
Black Eyes/GPS 2023 Open Poetry Competition

Christopher Horton

A Commuter Works at Home in the Village

Commuter, you're not supposed to be here during the working day
and, quite honestly, you don't know how the community ticks
when you're not here. Sure, this is where you moved
and you have given *the tour* to your brogue-clad friends
and met some of the *local characters* but you have not lived like this,
not in this time and space you were never meant to occupy.

If you want proof, witness the cafe where no one acknowledges you
or moves, much, except the waitress who looks knowingly anxious
when she takes your order for a skinny-flat-white
in her thick and ivy patterned notebook, or note the way
the butcher stops whistling when you smile in his direction.

Another example: recall the *quaint* pub where the drinkers stared
just beyond the rim of their tankards in complete silence
only to gossip with one another in hushed tones
as you turned the handle on your way out. You suspect,
as the panelled oak door shut behind you, they re-amplified
age old dialects you'd never possibly understand as they quoted
your funny city script, mimed your airs and graces.

The signs are telling you what to do. The streets are full of them.
A language of arrows, miniature human walking silhouettes,
other symbols, all combine for you to interpret as you go.
These too are not as they were. You could follow them for kicks
but they would always take you back to the same place,
from the place you started. You could talk to another *local*
but they would only tell you what they have rehearsed to tell you
before returning to their cosy fire-lit parlour rooms
and leaving you alone again, listening to the church bells
ringing just as they nearly always have and nearly always will.

Longlisted
Black Eyes/GPS 2023 Open Poetry Competition

Daphne M. Larner

A dish served cold

*She hung his suits on trees
all down the Avenue.
She stole his address book.
Arranged to meet
his V.I.P. business clients, for imagined sex-
if she liked the look of them.
Otherwise just for the thrill
of illicit meetings,
for lunch or dinner -she didn't care.
Talked about how hungry she was.
Their hands might travel up her legs,
making 'off the menu' suggestions.
More wine, playing for time,
then a pre-determined decision:
an exit with 'Please excuse me'
-they imagine 'The Ladies'.
Her coat might be abandoned
in the process of disappearing
through the kitchens.
A flirt with the chefs en route,
telling them to wrap her up
en croute - put her on the menu
for the next hungry punter
with money to spend
on a healthy appetite.
Outside the back entrance,
discreet, in a haze of steam,
and the lighting up of cigarettes -
a sudden short break,
taken by the curious,*

from their culinary duties-
she's seen waving for a taxi.
The trees on The Avenue
have shed his suits like leaves
but the pavements are clean.

'Commended'
The GPS Friendship Prize

Sally Aspden

After the moon

Overnight, a lake
has sprung from nowhere
on the Severn floodplain.
A huge shining lake
complete with seagulls bathing.

Yet it hasn't rained.
Some bewildered moments
until I twig:

Last night a full moon shone.
This morning's tide
pulled by moon and equinox
must have bored upstream,
spilled over, receded,
gifting an entire lake
gleaming in spring light.

Longlisted
Black Eyes/GPS 2023 Open Poetry Competition

Alan Mansell

A is ?

Planted in the centre of paradise
the fruit that brings all knowledge,
comes subtly recommended.

The refreshment of its flesh
cloaks the poison pips
of banishment.

It's second fall reveals hidden force
keeping spinning spheres
in their places.

The monster that lurks
in the daily diet
to scare clinicians away.

Market sold with free maths insight,
pencilled on the brown paper bag
in which a pound is twirled and wrapped.

The Revolution of a White Album,
changing worlds without big bang destruction,
turning at thirty three and a third.

A communication device, all knowing,
imparting it's "carefully selected recommendations",
now tracking my every move.

Longlisted
Black Eyes/GPS 2023 Open Poetry Competition

Claire James

A long way down the road

The roses she remembered. Their fragrance as much as form.
That book - a la recherche du temps perdu. And at the festival
Some still called christmas, what were they, the yellow ones,
Trumpeting an arrival? Daffodils - oh yes - which her mother
Had continued to describe as spring flowers, though seasons
Were already by then indistinguishable, a thing of the past.
Now there were no gardens. Or none permitted. Just a few
Clandestine corners. But the neighbourhood drones
Kept a close check, and the cost of water was prohibitive
Anyway. People showered, these days, just on a sunday.
It had been like that in previous ages, so much she knew,
Though the study of history was increasingly discouraged.
Occasionally though, momentarily subversive, she scraped
The gravel off her compacted soil and wondered, might
Anyone - despite the penalties - still have seeds for sale.

Longlisted, Shortlisted, 'Highly Commended'
Black Eyes/GPS 2023 Open Poetry Competition

Owen Gallagher

and when the children vomited

as they came out of the water
and tested positive
for sewerage
we complained bitterly to the guardians of the sea

and when fish threw themselves
out of the rivers
we wrote to the minister
who wrote to the water companies
who wrote to farmers
who all denied responsibility

and when they told us our bodies were full
of micro-plastics
from tap water
and eating fish
we took part in a medical research programme
that had links with oil and gas companies

and when the birds didn't know whether
it was safe to fish or land
on our shores
permits were granted to drill for profits
like there was no tomorrow
and our children in the classroom
were drawing life
as it could be

Longlisted
Black Eyes/GPS 2023 Open Poetry Competition

Carol Sheppard

Anglerfish

I wake to voices floating across the harbour:
clank of chains, soft chug of boats;
know before I open my eyes, you are gone.
I miss you.

I miss the way you held me in your arms
last night, your soft kisses on my skin,
how we melded together and it felt right.
We clung to each other as anemones

cling to rocks, begging the moon not to rise,
the tide not to turn. Melted into each other,
danced as high flung herring quiver
silver in moonlight.

How we lost our eyes, became blind,
our limbs and muscles merged,
your skin became my skin,
our blood shared the same veins.

Now in morning's wide yawn,
the screech of the black headed gull
cries from my own strangled throat.
My hand reaches and feels the chill

of the empty sheet, your scent drifts
away like a schooner chasing the waves.
I knew that the sea would call you back.
I miss you.

Longlisted
Black Eyes/GPS 2023 Open Poetry Competition

'Commended'
The GPS Friendship Prize

Vicky Hampton

Aubade

I think there were always meant to be violins.
From those first deep-tongued kisses
under the soaring walls of the Elan dams
where kites wheeled ether, reeling in
our hearts till we were up there with them
in praise, to now,

where a sky that's moved the moon
through its offices, has turned to rain.
A new and strange adagio
plays a repertoire of changing greys
keeping tune with the low bowing
of your sleeping breath.

I watch the rise and fall of the lovely umlaut
in the small of your back growing clearer
with the hour, and consider
the cadences of us:
I think we've reached, and passed now
the part where the lark was supposed to be ascending.

Longlisted
Black Eyes/GPS 2023 Open Poetry Competition

Emma Lord

Be Still, But Never Stop

The rage built; they could not place
the source, nor the reach, of their anger.
Volcanoes grew, upon twin foundations:
        consumption, and regurgitation
                of media
enabled by an apathetic society of followers
which would deny their existence.

As they stood, poised on the brink
of erupting, or remaining silent
the patriarchy turned …
its ego supported by men,
        supported by women.
sneering at the individuals
who sought to raze it.
And in revealing its face
they saw the target of their ire.

For a moment, they paused,
grounding emotions, while
circular roots reached to connect
with others who felt it too.
All the time building,
        building,
                drawing breath.

They were still,
but never stopped.

Longlisted
Black Eyes/GPS 2023 Open Poetry Competition

Margaret Royall

Becoming Eve

Cantatas swell in my heart;
thunderous roars from the wilderness
shattering the marrow of fragile bones.

Harpsichord cadences float on thin air;
déjà-vu moments finally released, threads of
lost film-spools behind closed eyelids.

I listen transfixed by the open window,
immerse myself in flashback and prolepsis.

Tides of salty tears stain the ivory keys of
my mouth
flushing out remnants of childhood's idyll.

Time alone is precious ...
life's elixir
uplifts the bruised psyche
I brood the naked power of Eve.

For a few blissful moments
Bach's music unites us...

I am she; she is me

We are one.

Longlisted
Black Eyes/GPS 2023 Open Poetry Competition

Jean Grimsey

Black crow laughing in the city heat

I flung open the window, let the fresh air in.
The sky was dark, the sun hidden,
the thunder rolled around the Cardiff hills.
There was a streak of lightning,
I counted - six seconds from flash to clap,
the storm was just above Rhwbina.
That was where he'd lived with his mam and dad.

The black crow perched
on the topmost branch of the tree
growing out of the car park concrete
fixed me with a mean eye,
cawed in laughter, then flew away.
Its wings flapped slowly as it caught
the rising heat thermals from the city.

I envied the crow its sense of self,
who I was had changed.

Longlisted
Black Eyes/GPS 2023 Open Poetry Competition

Frank McMahon

BOUND

They follow the threads of morning's light
to mourn the living, carry the double-weight
of loss. There are no obsequies or rituals
except the daily acts of love and obligation.
The mass of cordage grows, sinews weaken.

Words cannot be forged into a blade to cut
these cords or coined to purchase salve.
Sunset and dawn, sunset and dawn the black ribbons
unspool, unspool and coil around them.
There is no measure for this double-binding.

Longlisted
Black Eyes/GPS 2023 Open Poetry Competition

Alice Brooker

Brontë Falls

What a woman claims is sacred / especially when its coldness turns the hand to red / as though water was glass or some metaphorical mirror / each moss is damp and dangerous / I feel my feet curl around the threads of slime and cling / with a small and sturdy triumph / they adorn this braver, climber self with a mothering shade and drape me inside a green, unkissable hue / filth is damp and fresh and covering my limbs until / I am / that old idol Artemis with no way out at current / the water tickles me the way time does when it counts itself–

Everything I have truly loved let me love it first

Longlisted
Black Eyes/GPS 2023 Open Poetry Competition

David J. Costello

Church Gone
(After Church Going by Philip Larkin)

This is the mildewed body and
splintered bone of a church.
No summoning bell troubles
the cold ventricle at the centre
of this village's genuflected heart.
Only a silent pulpit punctuates
the white noise of nothing.
The roof slumps to a hammock
for noisy gulls and jackdaws.
They mute wind, filter out such light
that a different God would keep.
Apostles crumble in alcoves,
scabbed in filth their glassy avatars
are sickening the sun.
Only St Peter smiles, his broken mouth
yawning in its frame.

There is a reckoning here.
The faithless offspring of the graveyard's
tenants don't care for such things.
Even the ancient door is un-hinged.
Pevsner admired the buttressed walls,
Norman arches,
the long gone wood-carved screen.
His framed words hang
in the village pub like a holy relic.
No frame holds Larkin's words.
It isn't a village like that.

It isn't a village at all.
Unbuyable houses have grown in the fields.
The church wont survive what comes next.

Longlisted
Black Eyes/GPS 2023 Open Poetry Competition

Vivian E. Badoni

Code Talkers I

An archaic language
that has survived the test of time
by facing the judgment of manifestation destiny.

This language was thought
to be unpure,
useless,
and disgusting.

In reality,
It is a language of
pictures and
definitions.

A language that
saved
the very people who wanted it dead.
It became a sealed code
kept by the government,
a code that no one can know,
a secret that isn't to be told.

Until years after its creation
it was freed and shared to the public,
but wasn't included in history books.
Those who spoke Navajo and Hopi
gathered and shared their tales
of how they formed the Code Talkers
and helped win the war.

Longlisted
Black Eyes/GPS 2023 Open Poetry Competition

Nigel Kent

Cost of Austerity

The silver Mercedes van,
couldn't be discreet
in a street where
no-one owned a car:
it pulled a jeering crowd of kids,
deprived of entertainment,
drew neighbours' scornful
eyes to gaps in curtains,
their ears to cardboard walls
to sneer at our first taste
of jack-booted officialdom,
of doorstep demands,
of the sovereign power
of the printed word
that no lock in the land can withstand,
that emptied all mum's labelled jars
to salvage our faux-leather suite,
the colour telly nan had handed down,
dad's Praktica camera,
and left mum crumpled,
like the tissues in her fist,
whilst dad filled scraps of paper
with sums that wouldn't side with us.

The day of reckoning
had been delayed -
the van unfilled
when they departed -
yet the bailiff's men had left with
something more treasured
than anything we owned.

Longlisted
Black Eyes/GPS 2023 Open Poetry Competition

Emma Lord

Crow

Talons reach forward,
toes spread into
precision landing.
wire grip clutches
the headstone
as it settles.

Stationary beneath the yew
she watches it probe
moss which has grown
over the inscription,
obscuring numerals
chiselled with care
for someone who lingers
in yesterday's memories.

Rearranging its feathers,
it side-steps along the granite.
Gentle movements
reverential
as though sensing
that it perches
within consecrated land.

From under the tree
the observer remains still.
In silent appreciation
of the corvid, a noble
among avians.

A moment passes.
Before the crow dips,
launches, wings reaching
up and out as it rises.

And in that instant
crow and watcher
are gone.

A collective breath
sighs through the
graveyard grasses.
And the dead sleep.

Longlisted
Black Eyes/GPS 2023 Open Poetry Competition

Dani Hawkes

Dad

You left me behind with not only a fear of rejection,
But a fear of expression

A fear so deep that when I try to speak,
My mouth opens but it is silence that lingers

There could have been monologues,
About beauty, about strength, heartache and love

But you took those words with you,
And they were not yours to take

So now, what's left?
A head full of scrambled thoughts and beautiful moments left unsaid

Why is this my baggage to carry?
It should be yours.

Longlisted, Shortlisted
Black Eyes/GPS 2023 Open Poetry Competition

Lisa Kelly

Dear Merthyr

It's been a long time since I trundled Bambi-legged,
slinking down your spectral streets,
the valleys looming, surrounding me in shadow;
the sun rising at someone else's door.

My 'A's have shortened, and my 'R' doesn't roll like before.
Raspberry has become Raaaspberry
in some metamorphosis of just tryin' to be understood, innit?

Yet,
you linger in the lesser used words,
amusingly appearing in the vowels of 'gua-ca-mol-e'
or the additional syllable in 'may-or' and 'sol-di-er'.
A sudden exclamation of 'ych-a-fi' or 'navy wen'
explodes surprisingly.

Like, I'm modulating my verbs to fit the key of this life,
this place,
feeling my voice muted in the clipped syllables of speaking properly,
innit.

I hear my voice echo back at me across this flat English landscape,
unrecognisable,
and I long for home.

Longlisted, Shortlisted
Black Eyes/GPS 2023 Open Poetry Competition

Anna Saunders

Dear Poetry, last night I dreamt I spoke with my father

he said, honoured though he was
to be the subject of my verse,
he wanted me to change my aesthetic.
No more elegies, he said.

Poetry are you listening?
No more sorrow, he said
and outlawed melancholia, coffins, the relics of loss.

He said *remember me clicking my fingers to jazz,*
or curled up with a cherished book,
or the two of us, arm in arm, two tight links,
walking in the woods.

Dear Poetry, this means tears are out,
as are confessions of grief,
depictions of sickness,
or agonising last days.
Dear Poetry - no more laments.

Listen - he said *write of me in the garden,*
warm books resting in our laps,
our heads framed by honeysuckle.

Dear Poetry -
little heavens must now replace little hells.
Prepare yourself to contain

the trumpets of the flower,

their pink flush, ambrosial scent,
the blessing of sun on stone.

Longlisted, Shortlisted, 'Highly Commended'
Black Eyes/GPS 2023 Open Poetry Competition

Jenny Mitchell

Eating Curry Goat
(After Lynn Emanual)

Mother is cooking to remember her own mother,
who could fill the yard with hunger by the way
she sliced an onion, the secret being a sharp knife,
then talking to the pot so softly, the daughter
at her side could never hear the words, inhaled
the pungent odour. This was in the fifties when
their kitchen was an outdoor shack on soft Jamaican
ground, next to a three-room dump, foundations
strained by one hard-drinking man, twelve young –
four buried over several years in the back yard –
and my singular grandmother. Whispering to a pot,
ignoring her last child, she waited for the onions
to wilt, then added chopped tomatoes taken from
the garden – a tiny scrap of land next to the family
crop – white orchids so full-blown it was not hard
to sell corsages to the swanky tourists staying in
the glass hotels perched above white beaches close
to Kingston Harbour, the sea a coral dream swimming
out to indigo, sun a blazing coin above a radiant horizon.
Lord God! my granny wailed. *How come these whites
have so much cash and we live rough?* A wealth of
spices added next, never measured out, the names
of her dead children sung repeatedly, a hymn that rose
the more she stirred. Her daughter – my own mother –
longed to speak but held her tongue, stood back afraid
to feel a lash if mourning was disturbed. Meat
was added next – the billy goat made fat over a few
months, killed out in the yard – eight remaining

children holding back their tears or they might feel
a lick as the throat was cut, blood dripping in a pot.
Smoke filled the outdoor kitchen, made my mother
and her mother choke, fan the air, run to the open
door – a price they paid for eating curry goat.

Longlisted, Shortlisted
Black Eyes/GPS 2023 Open Poetry Competition

Catherine Baker

Falling for the moon

At dusk he'd taken to standing, leaning against the back door,
fag between his coal-mucky fingers, braces hanging loose,
shirt dimming to lavender, his eyes eel-black.

He stopped eating hot food, asking for cold potatoes, pickled onions,
hard boiled eggs, something pale and sleek to scrape up, quick.
He became delicate, sea ivory frail, light as a lapwing.

When clouds were fitful he stayed up to glimpse a fickle gleam.
He got to know the hold over tides and took to whispering the night shore,
becoming a cold creature, all spindrift and froth.

He was lost when he stood, naked in bladderwrack and dabberlocks,
skin ripping, flesh diluting green into rock pools, his bones swaying
into the arms of brittlestars and the moon shattering all around.

Longlisted
Black Eyes/GPS 2023 Open Poetry Competition

Allan Lake

Fardel's Bear

My Juliet has grown resentful of my Muse.
Eyelash in her ham omelette, plural's
apostrophe being pointlessly possessive.
I thought us all compatible, at least
tolerant of each other but No, not the case.
The case is a thorny, over-crowded
rose bed at times. A fecund calamity.
No need to confess to Beloved
that Muse and I conjoined at some
propitious hour, like cockcrow,
for a deep and meaningful.
One can trust her to sniff a tryst.
Here I am, blithely adoring them both
while Lovely is smelling competition,
the scent of bear all over me.

Longlisted, Shortlisted, 'Second Place'
Black Eyes/GPS 2023 Open Poetry Competition

Linda Ravenswood

Gloria holds my hand *en San Bernardino*

Erase when I speak   I'll change my name they won't know
I'm my father's daughter he doesn't even live here he's across
town in Burbank hardly ever comes by is he drunk
is he an NDN on a day pass who is that guy in the car with him
why does he need some Consigliere ride along
to give me a birthday present am I that hard to look at am I
that hard to say *mija* to   Erase when I speak don't go in the sun
mama says you'll end up looking like an N-word she so white
her skin shines blue   Erase when I speak the boys
on Westwood Boulevard say wetback when they drink
hot-dog-on-a-stick I'm in fabulous culottes so obvious
but who I am obvious even with my fine educated brain
top open to *les vagues* and brown as brown can be
thin *para un* wet rope in the Colorado if they left me by
the side of the road in Barstow don't they
they don't know who i am   *The girl she was a wet rope in water
we used her all summer she got in the back of the Jeep
and when she woke up in the Chevy she was already all over Texas*
she stayed a while by the almond farmers but then she came home
all rung out they dropped her in Sebastopol but she found her way
down Temecula again *once the desert always the desert*
Erase when she spoke   I think she's working a restaurant now
just like her father just like her father

Longlisted
Black Eyes/GPS 2023 Open Poetry Competition

B. Anne Adriaens

I am me

The woman is kind and knows what she's doing,
speaks reassuring whispers and leads me to the table.
I give her my grandmother's bracelet because

I want to be an artist.
I want to be a scientist.
I want to be me.

Her kitchen is like any other kitchen I've seen,
the same clean and organised clutter. Still,
I clutch my scrunched-up knickers in my fist.

I wanted him, his sweet smile
and warm hands — everything — but
not this. Not now.

She knows what she's doing and I close my eyes,
focus on the kettle boiling, the water sloshing,
the smell of soap, interrupted by a searing sadness.

I do not agree with my father.
I can be accomplished without producing a child.
I am more than a womb.

A trickle of blood down my thigh on the walk back:
it tickles, but not enough to take my mind off
the newfound void.

I tell myself I am the voice
of all the girls
spurned by the patriarchy.

My bed is a square refuge lined with stained linen,

a box for the fever that won't abate.
The woman knew what she was doing

and I knew the risks and the rules
voted into laws
as if I needed a purpose.

My mother stops looking for the heirloom at daybreak
and her words are a comfort that fades
when she pulls a clean sheet over my face.

Tucked in with fresh soil:
this may not be what I wanted,
but I am me. I am me.

Longlisted, Shortlisted
Black Eyes/GPS 2023 Open Poetry Competition

Simon Alderwick

…in alignment

Dissected hot dogs frying in a fishbowl.
The neighborhood azkals patrol the street.
Manga trees shade a basketball game.
A videoke star holds a high note like a trophy.

My Way, Buwan, Bed of Roses.
2 by 2 bottles collapse on the floor.

Chicken feet and cuts of pork laid out on charcoal.
A mother, babe in one arm, turns the sticks.
The older sister plays violin on the porch
as roosters jump into trees for the night.

Back from the sari-sari store with bottles of Red Horse,
the father kisses his fiance, puts a beer to his lips.

To the West, above the electric cable treeline,
the three pinpricks of Jupiter, Venus and Mars…

Longlisted, Shortlisted, 'Highly Commended'
Black Eyes/GPS 2023 Open Poetry Competition

'Winner'
The GPS Friendship Prize

Tess Biddington

In the November square, Kherson

Tatiana tells the camera she can *breathe again*

behind her
flower-sellers   their buckets
of chrysanthemum
are mobbed by winter-bundled babushkas
who embrace bouquets

stalks dripping trails across the paving
to the men in sandy fatigues
AK47s slung   barrels to the ground
fingers forming *rock on* for YouTube

Tatiana agrees with the reporter
                that yes
the flower sellers   are happy
very happy   as another explosion
of yellow blooms is taken
like a newborn to the liberators

her gaze diverts almost indifferent
                they were   she said
some of them   very friendly
with the Occupants
she cannot look into the camera

But for now   the reporter jauntily
points out the blue and yellow rippling icon
above the government offices

while the flower sellers
count their hryvnia
sluice the pavements
with their profitable buckets
             and go home

Longlisted
Black Eyes/GPS 2023 Open Poetry Competition

Charlotte Murray

Knotted Ribbon
'If someone has a grudge or hate against a person, to cause concern, worry and anxiety, bits of knotted black ribbon are left around the victim's house to be discovered over time so as to wear the victim down.' – Object 257, Museum of Witchcraft and Magic

a month before my breakdown
I start finding them

a scrunched-up strip of night
tucked into the pocket
of my favourite hoodie

a broken knuckle
flanked by tender scraps of skin
slipped in with my water bill

a paltry snake bloated
with its latest gorge
bobbing in the toilet bowl

I even pull one from my curry
a wilting mass of synthetic spinach
stewed to sourness

they bloom from the mouth
feed on the sweat of everyday
injustices

I gather them like daisies
my desperate
burden of proof

then meet with dismay
at the sight
of empty hands

Longlisted
Black Eyes/GPS 2023 Open Poetry Competition

Estelle Price

Learning to sing

Instead, let the breath enter your diaphragm

he tells the pubescent girl, who slouches
in the terraced house,
brisked there by her anxious mother
to learn how to sing.

Keep your shoulders down,
breathe into the sides of your blouse.
You are a balloon that must be filled.

For the first time she allows air to probe
- warm, coaxing, like a Southend sea in summer.
It courses down her windpipe, flows past a chest
where early buds, creamy camellias, are beginning
to form, finds its way to her unmapped core.

And again.
Hold it there while I count to ten.

Eyes closed she dives into the black
as if she is at a water park hurtling down a slide.
Her lungs struggle, the leftover breath demands
to be freed, ribs tighten
like a boy's grip on a girl's wrist.

They do this over and over.
She dizzes. Hands sit astride her belly
wanting to join in. At last he says –

Open your mouth and sing.

And what comes is woman-born,
birthed in the damp below a barnacled pier -

is the sound of childhood set adrift
in an estuary on a raft without a sail.

Good, he says, *You are ready for scales.*

Longlisted
Black Eyes/GPS 2023 Open Poetry Competition

Jodie Duffy

Lexicon

you pick words from conversations
like scattered daisies
twirl their stems back and forth
between your fingers
you gather them from stories
look at them from all sides
to seek their meanings

you stash words in your pockets
while you watch TV
rediscover them later
while we sit around the table for tea
when you ask me
I search for synonyms
draw examples in the air

not sure if my wonky sketches
are good enough
but somehow you define them
bring them out a few days later
subtle in their sparkle
casually placed in a sentence
as if they had always been there

Longlisted
Black Eyes/GPS 2023 Open Poetry Competition

Stuti Sinha

Meteors In The Night

We spin out of galactic gravel
into the vaulting vacuum of the night;
streak across a hammock of stars.
Emblazoned in glowing showers,
we set the nebula aflame;
        as fireball and light fall.

Smouldering alchemy is stamped
when skin grazes skin.
Until we fall over the horizon
dispersed to dust
in the dipping dark
        as fingerprints lost in space.

We become untraceable plots
on faded maps;
stolen light plucked
in ashes of the galaxies,
For we are ephemeral
        as meteors in the night.

Longlisted
Black Eyes/GPS 2023 Open Poetry Competition

Julie-Ann Rowell

Midsummer's Day, Orkney

Following a tractor on its way to bale.
They're riffling in our next-door field,
starlings strict in behind the dipping paddles.
Poppies flare in verges, draw me to their black hearts.
Wind ripples the hair of the green barley
grown for beremeal. Swallows chase food,
find insects we can't see. For hundreds
of years they've hunted invisible life.
The car takes a corner and veers,
oystercatcher eyes me, leaves slowly,
peep-ing as if to say, *you bystander*.
A tall daisy wreath in a passing garden.
If I'm on the move, everything is. Shapinsay
flattened like pressed dough. This day
is rising, our destination clear.
Then the short text to say you've died.

Beremeal is a type of flour produced only in Orkney.

Longlisted
Black Eyes/GPS 2023 Open Poetry Competition

Catherine Baker

Nest

She had been warm armed, curved by a man who smiled in Italian,
carving steps from the shore up to her rocky fields.
Gone this long time, to repent in Sorrento.

She named the baby for a Welsh princess, before she found the girl
was *twp* and would never amount to much. She hid her shame
in the house with her black bible and silver spoons.

When sheep shearers or hawkers called they glimpsed a pressed face
between the walls, like an unexpected wildflower. Unschooled, slow
and silly, Nest grew up squinting behind the veil of her mam's floral
apron.

A ferocity of malignancy committed the mother to salty soil.
Nest, clueless, took to the shore, her mother's coat hanging big.
She paddled the cold fish sea, ran from breakers,

climbed the dunes, threaded lousewort and thrift through
her coarse hair. Huddled in the marram, blinking amazed
at a wet summer's sandy loving.

She carried back mermaid's purses, dead crabs,
bladderwrack to reek on the dresser behind the china dogs.
She shopped, buying Mars bars, armfuls of cola, crisps,

wore a mini skirt, showing swollen, red knees,
told men about her lack of menstruation, let cruel women
lipstick her loose, thick lips.

After a turmoil of brutal, bloody heaves, nobody was more astonished
than Nest to see a baby. Nobody admitted knowledge. Nobody
claimed
the black-haired, sea-eyed, Roman-nosed boy.

He came up bright, significant in the swell of a simple love,
his mother's silver lining. He had his grandfather's stunning smile.
And, in time, fulfilled his thwarted grandmother's aspirations.

Longlisted, Shortlisted
Black Eyes/GPS 2023 Open Poetry Competition

Estelle Price

Nightfall in Nairobi

In Kenya, or any sister country close to the Equator,
danger slinks in at six when the sun sinks and night splays
herself across the sky. A girl walking through Kibera
must run past the shack where men are drunk
on *Changaa,* must hide her possibility behind a broken
door eating *ugali* with seven siblings and no mother.
From one year to the next, she must wait out
twelve hours (the length of the flight I will soon take
to watch my son play lacrosse in San Diego) reading
by the light of a solar lamp, never seeing Venus ride a lion
across the sky, a bow and arrow in her arms.
Not for her a *mzungu's* moonlit drive in the Masai Mara,
wrapped in a *shuka,* to hear the hyenas bay.
A girl in a slum is forbidden the night.

Note
changaa – home brewed spirit; *ugali* – cornmeal; *mzungu* – a white person; *shuku* – blanket

Longlisted
Black Eyes/GPS 2023 Open Poetry Competition

'Highly Commended'
The GPS Friendship Prize

Sharon Savory

No Country

Bone deep. Porous. Brittle.
There is no country.

One day the outside in
flips inside out and
Revelations stands
on a street corner
swearing on the bible.

The eyes of a raised
finger swing level
with a look that
seizes the question
the answers it:
squeezing it tightly in
judgement's fist.

With no shelter
there is no hiding.
Outside in:
this is Brixton
and they know
by the white of my eyes,
the brown of my skin

that I am nothing more
than spilt milk
and chocolate.

Bone deep, porous, brittle:
there is no country.

Longlisted
Black Eyes/GPS 2023 Open Poetry Competition

Iris Anne Lewis

Ode to Women Wielding Swords

Celebrated in the frescoes of Mycenae
two women stand in confrontation.
One, full-skirted but bare-breasted,
holds a spear; the other, caped
in full-length mantle, rests an imperious hand
on the pommel of a weighty sword.
She gestures towards two diminutive
and naked men floating in mid-air.
Their puny arms ward her off.
Their skinny bodies lean back
in defence.

Mortally wounded, lying by the waterside,
the leader of the Ancient Britons commands
his trusted knight to cast the royal battle sword
into the reed-strewn lake. The Lady lifts
her white-sheathed arm through the shimmer
of the water, catches the hilt. Three times
she brandishes the blood-glinting blade,
summoning a funeral barge. To the rhythm
of softly dipping oars the once and future king
glides through silken mist to rest
in deathless time.

In a thousand-year old abbey
a woman, clothed in turquoise
embroidered with glinting wreaths of fern,
bears a sword in a velvet-covered scabbard –
crimson embellished with silver-gilt.
She leads a docile king to the stripping
of his fur-trimmed robes to simple linen shift,
guides him to his enthronement.
Crowned and golden-cloaked,
he follows in her wake,
does her bidding.

Longlisted, Shortlisted, 'Third Place'
Black Eyes/GPS 2023 Open Poetry Competition

Emma Conally-Barklem

Philip Larkin meets Josephine Baker

There was something withered, as if he hung loose in nylon trousers and cotton shirt, malodorous. As if words had turned in the drabness and rolled in the febrile dirt under his stained fingernails.

She looked.

Her eyelashes feathered commas as if she was startled but she'd known filth herself.

She'd known how to make a negative out of personality then surprise with a splash of Belize black orchids so they'd say the word beginning with E with an X in the middle and she could suck her complexity in like an unlettered signing.

He smirked at once bemused and belligerent, his handkerchief caught the water from his eye which slid down the incline of her waist. **No bananas. But don't they all eat bananas or carry them in holsters to blackness to remind us it is we who are held hostage? Like I can't see**, he thought, and wondered how she arranged her linen.

The spark of her match cracked him to attention, her pupils dim in small flame bath. *Did you always write?* she asked, peach melba in her voice which welled from a throat cloved in Ermine.

Nonplussed, his eyes glazed, funny the question he longed for should come from a negro dancer.

Longlisted
Black Eyes/GPS 2023 Open Poetry Competition

James Lilliefors

Postlude
(For Janet)

In these summer woods, a postlude plays.
Ripe with melody, remembered phrase.
A call to rest by familiar trees,
To breathe the air of remembered days.

Magic you made despite the disease,
With ten fingers and eighty-eight keys.
Playing preludes and postludes akin.
But just the postlude gets a reprise.

Preludes were meant to draw people in,
Say welcome, let the service begin.
The postlude came with a deeper aim,
Not for the ear, for under the skin.

The song started slow, a minor chord
Stepped up to major, the chorus soared,
Then changed again, muse of many moods,
Echoing countries, keys you explored.

Time is spent this way: on long preludes,
on interludes, and circular feuds,
on breaking out of what might be chains,
but, more likely, are just attitudes.

Your song knows this, it nearly explains
The secrets of stars, hymns, autumn rains.
Song of color, cat-logic, D'Orsay.
Things that you loved, the song still contains.

So I pause in these old woods today
And listen. Awed by the swish and sway

Of wind and leaves, of beauty at play.
Two years to the day you went away,
a simple truth is still here, to find:
It's not what we make, take, win or say
That matters. It's what we leave behind.

Longlisted, Shortlisted
Black Eyes/GPS 2023 Open Poetry Competition

Paul Francis

PUTIN AND ME

He came to visit me today.
The young nurse said "That's nice of him."
"He came", I said, "to check I'm on my way.
I bet he won't attend my funeral. "

When we were young, I'd take her for a drive.
The fields stretched for ever, ripening wheat.
We'd watch the quails go mad. And so did we.

He thinks I killed the Union.
I worked so hard, tried everything
to save it, keep the dream alive.

The mountain is high, and there's a forest below...
I used to know so many poems by heart.

I was a teenage Stalinist.
I wrote an essay on him, won a prize.

"Don't make me angry, or I'll raise my hand."
Tears streamed down her face.
I understood. A bear. A stupid bear.

I climbed the ladder, read through all the files.
A nightmare, bleaker by the page.
If not me, who? If not now, when?

It was sclerotic. Tired men
who couldn't see things had to change.
"Who's planning for the future here?"

...there's a river, shining like a mirror...

Yes, I was overconfident.
Made deals that others didn't keep
and failed to spot conspiracies
but freedom is the key.
I wasn't wrong on that.

...towards the green valley, it's running away.

He called me soft.
Lock up the rebels. Show them who's in charge.
Be Russian. Forged in winter, hard and cold.

He called me henpecked. What I know is this:
my life lost meaning on the day she died.
The frozen fear of Stalin's not enough;
Russia is Pushkin and Rachmaninoff.
If you've loved someone, and been loved by them,
that matters more than rigged opinion polls.

Longlisted
Black Eyes/GPS 2023 Open Poetry Competition

Sharon Savory

Rainbows on the Shore

There is a man
hunting rainbows on the shore.
He thinks they slide
between the stoic rocks
on the backs of oblivious crabs.

Eyeing bearded mussels,
a gull's cry stutters
over the sanguine tongues
of those shoes, gripping
against death in the refracted

mark of the Moon. A halo falls
beneath his aqueous skin;
crabs shrug off possibility and
now, naked, watch a man sigh
with the weight of the tide

tapping the back
of the undigested imprint
in his unfinished painting.

Longlisted
Black Eyes/GPS 2023 Open Poetry Competition

Sue Finch

Raking for the Moon

It was not often
that you let me catch you
at the exact moment of being full.

Perhaps there was pleasure
in making me wait,
having me return again and again,
my eyes eagerly searching your sky.

Each time you were whole you had me awestruck,
as a crescent I loved you,
and when you were slung low in the sky
I threw all my wishes on you.

I remember vividly the night I took
some of your silver;
you had that bulge
which sometimes made me look away.

You were right overhead,
waning just a little,
with the exact same shape
that when you were waxing
made me tingle.

Maybe I didn't care so much
because it was the diminishing time.
Maybe I just got lucky.

All I know is, when I dipped
the rake into the river,
a part of you clung like weed.
I gasped when I saw it,
white on the horseshoe,

laughed as I hauled it in
to drop it in my jar.

I screwed the lid tightly
on this ghostly shadow of you.

Longlisted
Black Eyes/GPS 2023 Open Poetry Competition

Charlie Markwick

Reveal

It's always there that glass, tempting,
snidely offering self reflection. And
in these moments I weaken, allow
the lonely struggling thing inside to
look.

It's always there the hideous thing
that looks back from the glass. I
loath it, the deriding self, the
sneering me. The glass displays
contempt.

It's always there and every time I look
I smash the glass. But tyranny endures,
the mirror never breaks for long.
A thousand shattered shards mend and
mock.

The creature revels in my weakness,
my need to look. It whispers "the speculum
reveals what you truly are. End the torment,
rive the glass, take a precious shard and
slice.

"Tournous-Darré 13/08/23"

Longlisted, Shortlisted, 'Highly Commended'
Black Eyes/GPS 2023 Open Poetry Competition

Linda Ravenswood

sky of los feliz

I cannot refuse talking about the goats head
severed   but hanging in trees
a bees nest   a golden shuffling thing making a racket
a wasps den   where bets are laid   on who will be darkest
whose mate will lean longest
into the black-dark wine of love

                      all burned violins smoulder at the feet of this
                      contraption
                      this ache called a tree   this eye of the desert
                      this portal and hitching post   where we
                      made love under cover of night
                      whose leaves sang us our once and childhood
                      song
                      the ground so swollen with love and regret
                      we touched, made children, and goodbyes
                      our anthems racked our flags gone
                                          how the bees cover their
                                          queen how they rail her
                                          a buzz alight how they
                                          bring her their fluttering
                                          rakes and antennae to
                                          stitch-in beside her
                                          how they never leave
                                          her how they cover her
                                          to death and bring her
                                          over how they dance
                                          and beat upon her
                                          mask her with their low
                                          wings   how they cowl
                                          her with tongues in a
                                          desert song that trails a
                                          violent sarabande as
                                          they put her to bed the
                                          last time

Longlisted
Black Eyes/GPS 2023 Open Poetry Competition

Charlotte Faulconbridge

Slow Dancer

Don't eat your words,
They never taste good.
I would know,
I've swallowed a few.

I never thought,
I'd live to regret.
Words that I said,
When we first met:

*"I don't believe in love at first sight,
I don't find peace from spirits of the night,
I'm not one, for being a romancer."*

But you turned me into, *a slow dancer.*

Longlisted
Black Eyes/GPS 2023 Open Poetry Competition

Melvin Palowski Moore (Silver Lion Poet)

SOLDIER

I am a lion
Born
Of a beautiful legacy
With pride in my heart
And fire in my soul
I fought for all of us
But find that I am
Redlined
Torn, worn, threadbare
But not defeated
By shadows of darkening skies.
Inside me voices roar
Thunder rising
From stealing shackles.
I stand with my ancestors
Shouting!
Shouting!
Shouting!
I love my blackness
My people, my history
My country
That has not always
Loved me.

Longlisted
Black Eyes/GPS 2023 Open Poetry Competition

Simon Alderwick

speech therapy

Our language came down in the last rain,
meaning our meaning crawls and pulls
at the coattails of experience.

Always at its best when asking
What is this?

*

Our language came last of our senses.
An afterthought when our taste buds failed
to tell of danger, to separate
a legend from the shock of thunder.

*

Our language is flint and steel
struck in a cave.
Not light
but giver of light.

Our caves are full of books.
The TV, the stereo's on.
We have so many ways
to say we're not alone.

*

Our language is a river that goes nowhere,

a tangled knot,
a lump of ice in your whiskey throat.

Our language is as sweet
and melts as quickly
as nostalgia and memory.

Our language was invented
to describe things
that were born before us
and will outlive us all.

*

We must learn ancient curses
to honor the past

and pick up the cuss words
of the youth.

So that we, with bile flaming
in our stomachs, can pass
our story forwards,

in our own voices

our own truths.

Longlisted, Shortlisted
Black Eyes/GPS 2023 Open Poetry Competition

Dominic James

Station to Station

Headed back from Gloucester Station,
a feral pigeon on the track,
the overlong, spine of Platform One:

Keep it and welcome. I met no sense
of character at this cathedral stop.
No spark of Ivor Gurney's good report,

no surly duke, nor Doctor Foster stuck
into a puddle right up to his middle
in a shower of rain,

only those ordinary souls
of Philip Larkin's sort, for whom
it has become 'more difficult to find

words not untrue and not unkind;'
then hang my head in shame. Pulled up
short at Terminal Regret.

What have I done? One hard look,
an off-hand spite has bitten off the head,
torn to shreds domestic comfort.

And I am become passenger and victim
of my tongue. Depart. All change.
Take heart and run. Where to from here?

The ticket's stamped with 'Valid for',
'Restricted routes,' 'From and To.'
The land is wide and beckoning.

My train is bound for London Pad.,
I should alight by Valley Slad
but lines lead everywhere:

'Oh, Mr Porter,
what am I going to do?
I wanted to go to Birmingham
and ended up in Peru.'

I'll find white sand between my toes:
lose a shoe and find the Horn
of Africa. The glinting sea.

Before me thirsting, countless mouths
and eyes out-numbering
the random atoms of the air.

'I had not known there were so many'.
God knows you have been told.

Longlisted, Shortlisted, 'Highly Commended'
Black Eyes/GPS 2023 Open Poetry Competition

Alan Dunnett

Strict and Immovable

'It's beyond my control.'- Les Liaisons Dangereuses (Hampton/Laclos)

We apologise but we are constrained
by the parameters of the system.

What you've experienced is shameful but
there can be no exception for members
of the Windrush generation who fail
to qualify for citizenship here
through no fault of their own. Sorry. We're filled
with deep regret, for you lost everything.
Still, lessons have been learned and our approach
will change. It is quite true you could not work.
You were separated from your children.
We should have shown more flexibility.

We apologise but we are constrained
by the parameters of the system.

Informed by an Amelia Gentleman article – 'Windrush victim denied citizenship despite admission of error' - which appeared in 'The Guardian' 6 March 2021. A lot of its words, as revealed in the article, are from letters written by two home secretaries to a Windrush victim.

Longlisted
Black Eyes/GPS 2023 Open Poetry Competition

David Hale

The Birdscarer
Charles Baglin aged 8
sentenced to 4 days hard labour for stealing apples,
Horsley 1836

Up when larks
call the hare from its bed
you spend days

patrolling Long-Leaze
and Lagger
armed with a slingshot

and voice like a rattle
for scaring the scatter
and taunt of crows.

All week in wind and rain
for a shilling a day.
Is it any wonder

when your stomach aches
you dream of pippins
stored in Pegler's barn?

For a boy hears things
out in the fields,
hunger breeds distraction

and distraction leads
to a breach in the drystone.
Is it any wonder

a boy stealing apples
might grow careless
if the habit grows on him,

he gets four days hard
if caught red-handed,
a taste of the Turnkey's lash?

Longlisted
Black Eyes/GPS 2023 Open Poetry Competition

Nigel Kent

The Comfort of Crumbs

When the weather turns vigilante
and drives Hope from the city's streets
she shelters in Rosa's Café
where they let her linger
over complementary cake,
eavesdropping on the chatter
of customers that wraps its arms
around her shoulders
as she gathers up
the scraps they drop
of little Harry's pranks,
of Lee and Beth's engagement
of Paul's deserved promotion:
scraps that sustain her
throughout the cardboard-night,
stories projected on shuttered lids,
a box-set of happy endings
more warming than the hottest
Sally Army soup.

Longlisted
Black Eyes/GPS 2023 Open Poetry Competition

Jane Burn

The Effects of Rage
After Storm Arwen, 26/27th November, 2021

Arwen came / pain between her teeth
   her name enough / to make the sound
of wrath / against this broken land /
       she told herself to us / in ways of massive ire
   we feared at the windows / like crated pigs
  afraid of whipcrack wire
       here is Bible / ! / *says I* /   *Armageddon* /
  brought on the tongue / of a storm
air became the shape / of knives / the shape
    of lump hammering /   *cruel* / *with fury*
  much will fall / before her squall's sight
bough and trunk / a puny tinder of boundary gate
     trampolines orbiting estates /   their lost moons / curious
upon a stranger's churned lawn / birds flayed from the sky
  rage / rage against the dying of the light / I threw her some words
   how else might one placate / such a rampant beast / ? /
     she ate the sound of poetry /   from the keen screech
of my own voice / gored my skin / with hurtled ice
  goaded the night / with thorny crowns of snow
come with your worst /   *hooligan*   / I shout my own waste
against her / match her in this moment / crazed and wild
   my eyes / my shoes / my rage /
hold onto my house / claim it from her screaming fist
she is gnawing at the gable end /   *we're not in Kansas anymore*
    I defy this / scission / of her vicious breath
      defy her need / to break what I have built

Longlisted
Black Eyes/GPS 2023 Open Poetry Competition

Estelle Price

The mirror turns

black. The room revolves, orange silk becomes
green corduroy. Her legs grow hands.
A fox runs backwards across the lawn. In another country
people take off their clothes. On another
planet gold rivers start to flow. The Lord's Prayer begins
with Amen. A child is untied. Tarmac peels away
from earth like burnt skin and a blackbird returns
to its nest, reverts to egg. Salmon grow wings, fly away
from the river's source. Her thoughts become coin, sink
into bulrushes. Fallen leaves float up from the lawn,
grief-balloons that disappear at the horizon. All this on the day
her mother dies. And on her fingertip a ladybird.

(with thanks to John McCullough for the line – 'And on her fingertip a ladybird')

Longlisted
Black Eyes/GPS 2023 Open Poetry Competition

Annie Ellis

The Music Box

She sits alone
holding a music box
given by her father.

She turns the key slowly,
opening the lid
a ballerina in a pink tutu
pops up on tiptoe.

As the tinkling notes begin
the dancer turns a pirouette
again and again.

Tears fall from a face
as thoughts of her mother
dance into place.

'Mentioned'
The GPS Friendship Prize

Annie Ellis

The Scarf

Dragonflies billow light in a breeze
between folds of palest blue silk.
Every move she made sent them flying,
could they ever break free?

Their wings were translucent,
bodies shimmered like jewels.
Was it her perfume of lavender,
that held them spellbound?

Longlisted
Black Eyes/GPS 2023 Open Poetry Competition

Suzy Aspell

there's all the blue and all the green
(after 'Blue and Green Music' by Georgia O Keefe)

insects embedded in amber
we dream night after night
sleep cleaning our brains
removing all the blue and green
tomorrow there will be fresh music

sky and ocean are green
only our hearts are blue
there's heather on the wind
and midnight in lightning
thunder booms beneath our feet
we try to close the doors
the sky is breaking in
and we do not have the room
to hold it all in

tomorrow there will be fresh music
removing all the blue and green
sleep cleaning our brains
we dream night after night
insects embedded in amber

Longlisted, Shortlisted
Black Eyes/GPS 2023 Open Poetry Competition

Scott Elder

This

A 'Golden Shovel' after Martin Luther King Jr's
'Mountaintop' speech 1968

is the troublesome hour when only
Sleep runs free   when the wolf is in
and you are in   this is the
broken hour   when darkness
bares a fragile edge   this is you
and you again   no blink can
keep a wolf at bay   only *it* can see
or scent your breath   in the
restless whispers of wind and stars

Longlisted
Black Eyes/GPS 2023 Open Poetry Competition

Clive Oseman

THOUGHTS

The thought police thought
he thought thoughts he wasn't ought to
arrested him and tested him
messed with his head
till he wished he was dead
and confessed because he thought it best.

They could never have proved it of course.
It wouldn't have held up in an unbiased court.
Lack of evidence, there's no debate
but he took the bait and sealed his fate.

Truth is he was guilty under the law as it stood
because it has to be understood
that the right had been in power too long
and the masses knew where they belonged.

First peaceful protest was outlawed,
progressive thinking was abhorred
and the government controlled what teachers taught
what the TV said and what readers read.

The people could have halted this
but chance after chance after chance was missed
because few believed it could ever happen,
couldn't see the developing pattern.

The bastards laughed as their lies were bought.

It's too late now for dangerous thoughts.

Longlisted, Shortlisted
Black Eyes/GPS 2023 Open Poetry Competition

Isabella Mead

TOADSTOOL, FROG'S UMBRELLA

The man I love teaches me his favourite word
in Bengali: banger chatta / toadstool / frog's umbrella

and now we tread carefully in the forest
in case frogs are gathering ahead of rain,

or sunlight, when they might stretch out in the shade
under parasols. Science taught me little of sun and rain,

aside from life cycles and changing seasons,
tadpole to frog, and round again.

History lessons were perpetually sunlight through rain.
I learned that Churchill implemented naval reforms

as First Lord of the Admiralty, that as Prime Minister
he stirred the nation and rubbished talk of surrender,

that his strategy led to the defeat of Germany,
that he won the Nobel Prize for Literature,

never that he replenished British soldiers
from Bengal fields and rivers, while the others

looked on as their fruits of sun and rain
vanished altogether. There were never

any leftovers. I learned the number
and species of fungus. I learned that some

are hallucinogenic. I learned that toadstools
can be poisonous, but I never

pictured a relaxed toad putting his feet up,
crushing his brothers. I tell the man I love

I am moved by this.
By the poetry of the semantics, he notices,

not by those brothers. I punch him lightly. We laugh.
We are out together, foraging for mushrooms, in love.

Sometimes I slip on wet grass, sometimes he does.
We navigate rain and sunlight between us.

Longlisted
Black Eyes/GPS 2023 Open Poetry Competition

Anne Sheppard

Tomorrow I will Grieve for my Country

Last month I laid out the suit
That my son would wear for his wedding,
I brushed it and hung it up,
Admiring the quality of the cloth.
He had worked hard and paid
Good money to buy the best.

Last week I folded the suit
Into a leather suitcase, that I hid
Under old rags behind the boiler
In my brother's outhouse.
The Russians had arrived and I
Wanted to keep it safe.

Yesterday I buried the suit
Along with the remains of my son,
Who fought for us all - his family,
His bride to be, his future and ours.
I remembered with tears - his birth, his smile,
His last loving embrace.

Today I grieve for my son,
Tomorrow I will grieve for my country,
I will not be alone.

Longlisted
Black Eyes/GPS 2023 Open Poetry Competition

Maria Roe

Two Mirrors
Self-Portrait as the Allegory of Painting (La Pittura) - Artemisia Gentilleschi
Royal Collection Trust

Damp seeps inside my veins, cold air
clamps my chest.
The walls of my room are painted Tuscan brown
but the void is too chilled to be my home.
The lack of light
frustrates and challenges.
Where I work
is as basic as a monk's cell
and thoughts circle like this buzzing fly
battering the window.

I see myself from different angles.
Two mirrors show the hidden side.
The part my father is unsettled by,
the part he does not know.
Through my palette and brush
my shape surprises; my chin is proud,
my reach goes far.
My hands have the confidence,
dare I say it, of a man.

Before me is the person who I really am.
The search is nearing an end when I paint
with the utmost care to capture that fleeting
moment of truth,
I am at peace.
I rest a moment,
here in this damp cold room.
All is still and silent
and the fly has settled.

Longlisted, Shortlisted, 'Winner'
Black Eyes/GPS 2023 Open Poetry Competition

Charlotte Stokes Meyer zu Natrup

We dug a hole

There was something wrong with the language. When we drank it, it corrupted our lungs and we couldn't button it correctly. We approached it but it created traffic and twitched its territories on the tarmac. When we pruned it, it obscured the sky and when we cut it, it gave us indigestion and kept us up at night with a debris of bird song in a sky that was not quiet. When we schooled it, it smeared itself across our lips and could not be wiped away.

There was something wrong with the language. When we recorded its bodily fluids, it put its out of office on and graffitied its eyelids, its cheeks. We tried to measure it but it grew pain like moss on its south facing side and fell like grains of rice from bridges in the distance. We wanted to reassure it but it married inappropriately and changed the locks. At night, it poured a heartbeat into a sound that it listened to over and over and over so that we could not sleep.

There was something wrong with the language. We pet it, but it got food poisoning and spat teeth. When we tried to drive it, it used its fists to dial the emergency service and let its breath turn to glass. We sketched its likeness, but its wheels slipped on oil and it stopped believing in colour.

We couldn't be sure that it would not still-life the stock market, uproot the clouds and when its tears began to taste of sarcasm, we took its photo and dug a hole

Longlisted, Shortlisted
Black Eyes/GPS 2023 Open Poetry Competition

David Hale

Wimblebarrow

Tugged from the belly of Shortwood
three centuries back
he sprawls down the ridge,
navel pierced by a ring
of incandescent hawthorns.

In stark contrast to his neighbour
who's blade-bitten
and leached by his habit,
his unsprayed acreage
supports vole, beetle, barn-owl,

all summer hums to the tune
of a hundred-thousand hungry voices.
When snow dusts then drifts,
the moon-horned cows
that browse his flanks

are driven down to their sheds,
he settles beneath a quilt
of dung, mud and fallen leaves,
turns his face inwards
and travels into the darkness.

Longlisted
Black Eyes/GPS 2023 Open Poetry Competition

Jane Spray

Wing Mirror Love Song - A golden shovel after Bob Dylan

You're my offside wing mirror, baby. Sorry if
it pains you; I can see it may not

sound too glamourous, but then, what's a soulmate for?
Life's scary sometimes. I don't want to alarm or harm you

only to cwtch you, tuck you in towards me, safe in my
hands, through the narrow passes. I won't let the sky

dazzle you, the ground grime you, that would
never do. You reflect things, levelly. If we ever did fall

into the dark space of catastrophic rain
I know you wouldn't panic. You would

just demist yourself, tip me the wink. I'd gather
myself together. Perhaps I could be your mirror, too.

I couldn't face this journey without
you there beside me, without your

clear perspectives. You, doing what you love
without thinking about it; shining on. I'd

be the first to admit, without you I'd be
lost, my mojo gone; off road, going nowhere.

For everything relies on something else: at
the top of a pineapple another pineapple plant grows; all

the way up, it's pineapples; this song is a pineapple. Oh
and you are my nearside mirror too, lovely, that's what

I see now. Before I signal to go anywhere, you would
have me look into your depths and distances, and I

I'm happy to oblige, there's nothing I would rather do.
You're my two wing mirrors, darling; I rely on you. Sorry if

it pains you sometimes, to be attached and not
completely free – but isn't that a fantasy? I must watch out for

our blinds spots. Along with my rear view, I put such faith in you.

Longlisted
Black Eyes/GPS 2023 Open Poetry Competition

Greg Smith

Words Fail

But there is always something else:
in the doctor's waiting room, between the coughing

and the calling out of names, in museums,
beyond the still air sealed in each glass case,

in library aisles, past all the thought and drama
pressed between the pages.

Left alone with it, you must divert your mind's ear,
search your mobile for some answer,

small-talk over it or just drum your fingers.
If you stop to listen, it might swallow you.

In reverberating churches, voices drown it out;
the organ flooding the heft of stone.

The choir lays out a tapestry of vowels
as if defying it, but it is still there

in the niches and behind sarcophagi,
beneath the flagstones and below ribbed vaults,

beside the bedside priest,
between each questioning syllable of prayer.

At the cenotaph you can hold out
two whole minutes, stare at your feet,

try to think of anything; breathe again
when it is broken by the guns.

The Trawler Series

The Trawler Series are anthologies of poems trawled from the Gloucestershire Poetry Society (GPS) group Facebook pages.

The Trawler 2022 is the third and final edition in the trawler series, there was always only going to be three.

Some of these poems may be rough first drafts, still in need of polishing (we have only lightly edited) but never the less they are of sufficient value to be included within the pages of these anthologies.

Some are by published poets, and some by people who have just begun writing, being published for the first time, but each poem has an element: a style, voice or passion that called to us as we read it.

www.ingramcontent.com/pod-product-compliance
Lightning Source LLC
Chambersburg PA
CBHW052102110526
44591CB00013B/2317